Barney Norris

NIGHTFALL

OBERON BOOKS
LONDON

WWW.OBERONBOOKS.COM

First published in 2018 by Oberon Books Ltd
521 Caledonian Road, London N7 9RH
Tel: +44 (0) 20 7607 3637 / Fax: +44 (0) 20 7607 3629
e-mail: info@oberonbooks.com
www.oberonbooks.com

A catalogue record for this book is available from the British Library.

PB ISBN: 9781786823182
E ISBN: 9781786824929

Cover Design & Art Direction by Koto
Cover Photography by Chris Mosey

Printed and bound by 4EDGE Limited, Hockley, Essex, UK.
eBook conversion by CPI Group (UK) Ltd, Croydon, CR0 4YY.

Visit www.oberonbooks.com to read more about all our books and to buy them. You will also find features, author interviews and news of any author events, and you can sign up for e-newsletters so that you're always first to hear about our new releases.

Printed on FSC accredited paper

Samuel French Bookshop
At The Royal Court Theatre
Sloane Square
London SW1W 8AS
ph : 020 7565 5024

QTY	SKU	PRICE
1 N	9781786823182	9.98
	NIGHTFALL	
	(£9.99 each)	
	10% Discount	-1.00

Total Sale		£8.99
VAT		£0.00
Net Sale		£8.99
Credit Card		£8.99

Total of Discounts £1.00

THANK YOU FOR SHOPPING AT
SAMUEL FRENCH LTD
VISIT US
AT
www.samuelfrench.co.uk

VAT NO. GB 241
1290 07

Sale Date: 01/06/2018
Register: 1
Store: 2
Cashier: POS
Items: 1 Quantity: 1

Thank You For Shopping
at Samuel French Ltd
Visit Us at www.samuelfrench.co.uk

Vat No : GB 241 1290 07

01/06/2018 13:48:48

0000019854

For Hayden.

i.m. Margaret 'Peggy' Norris

O as I was young and easy in the mercy of his means,
Time held me green and dying
Though I sang in my chains like the sea.

Characters

RYAN
A farmer, 20s

LOU
Ryan's younger sister, 20s

PETE
Underwater welder, 20s

JENNY
Ryan and Lou's mum, 50s

The action takes place in the garden of a
Hampshire farmhouse.

Nightfall premiered at the Bridge Theatre, London, on 1 May 2018, with the following cast in order of speaking:

Ophelia Lovibond – LOU
Sion Daniel Young – RYAN
Ukweli Roach – PETE
Claire Skinner – JENNY

Director, Laurie Sansom
Designer, Rae Smith
Sound Designer, Christopher Shutt
Lighting Designer, Chris Davey
Music, Gareth Williams
Video Designer, Ian William Galloway

This text went to press before the end of rehearsals and as such may differ from the play as performed.

Act One

SCENE ONE

A farm, late evening, almost dark. Night will fall across the course of the scene. An oil pipe runs across the stage, raised on struts above the ground so it stays level on its journey from Fawley up to Birmingham. There's a septic tank at the edge of the stage. PETE wears a welding mask and carries a welding iron. RYAN watches him. PETE fires his welding iron, and a light jumps into the sky. PETE goes to work on the silage tank. He's sealing in a tap he's just installed. From the other side of the stage LOU watches them, sipping on a bottle.

LOU: And there's no way anyone's ever gonna know?

RYAN: It's totally safe, Lou. Pipe like this loses gallons already. This runs for like a hundred miles, right? So you get leaks and dirt, loads of wastage. Sometimes it runs underground, and then you've got ploughing or roadworks. Then above ground there's corrosion. Or someone'll drive into it.

LOU: Or pikey lads might tap it and siphon some off.

RYAN: It's not pikey.

LOU: No, just fucking reckless. Has he got it?

PETE has lifted his visor.

RYAN: Safeways here we come!

PETE dumps his welding gear on the ground.

PETE: You got it then?

RYAN grabs a metal object to be screwed onto the pipe, and passes it to PETE.

RYAN: Oh yeah.

LOU: Oi Pete your arse is hanging out!

PETE: What?

LOU: *(Laughing at her joke.)* No don't worry.

PETE: Was my arse hanging out?

LOU: No, it was a joke. Cos you both look sort of like builders. And builders always have their arses out. Don't worry.

PETE: You know this is basically what I do for a living?

LOU: Is it? I thought you did skilled work.

PETE: This is skilled work.

LOU: Doesn't look it.

PETE: That's cos I'm doing it badly. I'll get this on.

RYAN: Woo!

PETE: Keep your tits on, work environment.

RYAN: Sorry.

PETE: This is a fucking SAS mission, remember. Special Forces shit.

RYAN: *Gears of War.*

PETE: Not *Gears of War*, for real.

LOU: X Box monkey.

RYAN: Fuck off.

PETE: It's on.

RYAN: Woo!

LOU: Getting proper dark now.

PETE: Don't worry. Wasn't in scouts for nothing. Hashtag prepared.

PETE fishes about in his pocket, takes out a head torch, puts it on and turns it on.

LOU: Is that the scout motto?

PETE: No, that's Durex.

LOU: Surprised you know that one, with your latex allergy.

PETE: My latex allergy is not a laughing matter.

LOU: Course not.

RYAN: You look proper Duke of Edinburgh.

PETE: Think that's when I bought it. Shall we do this?

RYAN: Fuck yeah!

> *PETE sets to piercing the pipe by turning a massive spanner that's tightening the bit of metal he's just attached.*

LOU: How much is it gonna make us then?

RYAN: I dunno like, loads. Don't worry about it.

PETE: Ryan this is too hard, you have to –

RYAN: Oh right, sorry.

> *They work on turning the big spanner together.*

RYAN: That it?

PETE: That's good. Right, and we have to –

> *The pipe is pierced, oil pours over them.*

RYAN: Shit!

> *They tighten the valve*

PETE: OK. Cool. We're fine. We're fucking fine.

RYAN: Let's have a goosey?

PETE: It's gander, you can't say goosey.

RYAN: You can say either.

PETE: You can't, it's gander. You stay back yeah?

LOU: If he's having a look I'm having a look.

PETE: It's dangerous.

LOU: You're a sexist pig.

PETE: No, I just mind less if he gets horrifically disfigured than if you do.

RYAN: Looking good, mate.

LOU: For the work of a sexist pig.

PETE: Right, hose on.

RYAN: Cool.

RYAN grabs the hose that's attached at one end to the septic tank.

RYAN: Fuck me, that's heavy.

PETE: Gotta use the proper gear.

RYAN: Jesus.

PETE: Tell you what, further back. You hold it there, and I'll –

RYAN: All right, yeah.

RYAN takes hold of the tubing further back.

PETE: You could help a bit maybe Lou.

LOU: Yeah?

PETE: Get that bit.

LOU goes to the middle of the hose and helps.

LOU: Just keep doing that?

PETE: Go slow, I gotta get it – yeah, that's sweet.

LOU: You know Mum'll freak when she sees it.

RYAN: Yeah, but I run the farm now. I'm in charge, she agreed that, I choose what we do. And this is a chance to give ourselves an edge, so I wanna take it. This is life, Lou. You need to take what you can get, or there will be fuck all for you. You there?

PETE: Yeah.

RYAN: This is so fucking exciting!

PETE: Stop shouting Ryan, focus.

RYAN: All right.

PETE: Have a pull on that then.

RYAN gives the hose a tug at the septic tank end.

RYAN: Sorted.

LOU: It's not gonna come out?

RYAN: All good.

PETE: All right then.

PETE opens the valve so oil can pass through the hose while the other two are talking, checks it doesn't fall off and disentangles himself from the pipe before going back round to the front of the septic tank to test his work.

RYAN: Think about how our lives might change. That's what matters. We could go back to Lanzarote if we had a bit of money. Or Beefa.

LOU: I don't think I'd go back to Lanzarote without Dad.

RYAN: It's different for you. I'm up to my neck, you're only here till you move back out. Mum and Dad had their whole lives to make this place work, and we live on fish fingers and beans. I'm done with that. My turn now.

PETE: It's done.

RYAN: Let's see?

PETE turns the tap and oil comes out. Both lads go mental.

RYAN: Woo! Thank you, mate. I need a drink I reckon.

LOU: You're both covered in shit, you know that?

PETE: We are a bit, aren't we.

RYAN: You got a change of clothes with you?

PETE: Inside.

LOU: You're not going in like that, she'll murder you.

RYAN: He can do what he wants, he's sorting us out.

PETE: Yeah, Lou. You used to be much more grateful when I sorted you out.

LOU: So inappropriate.

PETE: Fair enough.

PETE starts undressing.

LOU: Seriously?

PETE: Well if I can't go in with my gear on.

LOU: Fuck's sake.

PETE: What?

LOU: Nothing. You and all then. You're the one who shits yourself on nights out and walks it up the stairs.

RYAN starts undressing.

RYAN: That's not true.

LOU: It's literally true and you know it.

RYAN: I was getting in the shower to clean my jeans, how else was I gonna clean my jeans?

PETE: Better bin this lot.

RYAN: Yeah?

PETE: It won't come out.

They've undressed. They dump their things on the floor.

LOU: Quite a Vladimir Putin look going on.

PETE: Personal style icon. You got another cider?

LOU: Yeah.

LOU chucks PETE a cider and he opens it.

RYAN: We not going in?

PETE: In a sec. Quite like it out here like this, I feel like a wild man. Like a bear.

LOU: You should be aware you both look significantly less cool than you think you do.

RYAN: Can I have a bottle and all?

LOU hands RYAN a beer and he opens it.

RYAN: Ta. Well. This is awkward.

PETE: Why? Lou always liked me with my shirt off.

LOU: Fuck off.

RYAN: Told you.

He sips his cider.

PETE: I know what you're thinking about.

LOU: What?

PETE: You know.

LOU: No.

PETE: You know!

LOU: You're being boring.

PETE: All right. Strip poker.

RYAN: Really?

PETE: Lou used to love strip poker.

RYAN: Erm –

PETE: Which was weird, considering how bad you were at it. Used to skive off college and play it in her room, and you barely seemed to know the rules sometimes. I'd still have my blazer on and you'd be –

LOU: Well sometimes if your boyfriend's always saying how tired he is a girl has to try and get things moving for herself, you know?

RYAN: I might just leave you to it I think.

LOU: You fucking won't.

RYAN: All right. I don't even know how to play poker. Probably cos I didn't spend the whole of college fucking around playing cards.

PETE: To be fair, we didn't play a lot of cards.

RYAN: I was too busy getting an actual qualification, wasn't I.

PETE: What, swimming badges? Cycling proficiency?

LOU: Tractor driving for beginners?

RYAN: I'm not fucking thick. I know shit.

PETE: *(Sings.)* I can't read, I can't write, it doesn't really matter, cos my name's Ryan and I can drive a tractor!

RYAN: I know shit.

LOU: What?

RYAN: I dunno. D'you two know any constellations?

PETE: I'm not a fucking hippy, Ryan.

RYAN: All right.

PETE: Constellations, fuck off. I don't know my star sign and I haven't got dream catchers over my bed.

LOU: No, you've got Fraser Forster.

PETE: Still remember that then?

RYAN: Well I learned some. Orion and whatever.

PETE: Oh yeah?

RYAN: It's quite cool actually.

PETE: Oh right?

RYAN: They move around up there, that's cool.

PETE: Do they?

RYAN: Yeah.

LOU: Well they don't. They stay still, the earth rotates.

RYAN: Oh, yeah. Same thing. Main thing is that I've noticed if I leave the Fisher's Pond at eleven, Orion's right over the house when I park the car. But if I've been out clubbing or whatever, and come back in a cab, he's fucked off somewhere else. Isn't that great?

LOU: You're an idiot.

RYAN: Why?

LOU: You only chat like that when he's around, I'd forgotten you did this.

RYAN: What?

LOU: You know.

RYAN: No, what?

LOU: Shut up.

RYAN: What, Lou?

Beat.

PETE: I've got a joke.

RYAN: Go on.

PETE: This bloke was conducting this orchestra. Foreign bloke, didn't have that much English, and it turned out he wasn't much good at conducting either, all the musicians thought he was a right twat. And they were in their last rehearsal before some big gig, and everything was going to shit, you know? So this dude decided to read them the riot act. Really snap 'em together. And he called them all together and had a go, except his English fucked him over.

RYAN: Go on, what did he say?

PETE: He stood in front of them all. Shoulders back. Magisterial. And he looked down at them all, and they're looking at him like, who the fuck are you? And he said to them, you think I know fuck nothing. But I tell you now, I know fuck all! True story.

RYAN: That's quite good.

PETE: True story. I didn't mean to be a dick about all dream catchers, mate. Didn't know you were into it.

RYAN: You're all right.

PETE: Sorry. It is interesting. Just not the sort of thing you talk about inside, you know?

RYAN: Sure, yeah, sure.

PETE: But it is interesting. You can work out where north is and whatever, can't you.

RYAN: Yeah, exactly, yeah.

PETE: What other ones d'you know then?

RYAN: I only really know Orion. I know some names, the Plough and the Bear and whatever, but I've only looked at diagrams, I don't really know what they look like.

LOU: Plough and a bear, probably.

RYAN: Yeah, but can you see that up there? They all just look like stars to me.

LOU: Sound like pub names don't they.

RYAN: D'you think there's a constellation called the Dog and Duck?

RYAN and PETE laugh.

PETE: Tell you what, that might be the Fox and Hounds though.

RYAN: Yeah?

PETE: That bright one there, that's the fox. And all the other fucking stars, that's fucking millions of hounds.

They laugh.

RYAN: Yeah. All right Lou? You had enough of us?

LOU: No, just. In a stare, you know? You ever go into a stare? Like a little coma. There was this thing on the news. Someone dug up a septic tank in a field on the edge of a children's home in Ireland. This half buried septic tank, wasn't connected to anything. I don't think it was connected up. And this orphanage was run by the church, obviously, cos it dated from whenever and everything used to be run by the church. And they cracked the thing open and found the skeletons of like, two hundred children inside.

PETE: Fuck me.

LOU: I know right?

RYAN: Why are you telling us that?

LOU: Dunno. You know. The shit you find on farms.

PETE: You said it was an orphanage.

LOU: All right, the shit people do with septic tanks.

PETE: What's the difference between a bowling ball and a dead baby?

RYAN: Mate.

PETE: You used to laugh at that.

RYAN: In school. Real world now, innit, you can't do dead baby jokes.

PETE: Yeah, all right, sorry. It is a bit funny though.

LOU: It's really not.

PETE: Always liked a joke, you and me. What's funnier than a dead baby in a clown suit? Oh, wait, no, I've got that wrong.

LOU: You're disgusting.

The sound of a car parking. Lights strafe their faces.

LOU: That Mum?

RYAN: Shit.

LOU: She seen us?

RYAN: Thought she was back tomorrow?

LOU: Yeah, me too.

RYAN: Oh, fuck.

Enter JENNY.

JENNY: All right Pete.

PETE: All right Jenny. How's erm, how's things?

JENNY: What's going on here?

RYAN: Pete's been helping me sort some broken gear.

JENNY: What's that hosepipe?

RYAN: That? That's something we're mending.

JENNY: What are you doing?

RYAN: Well, it's an idea we had. What we're doing right, what we're doing is siphoning a bit of spare oil out of this pipe into this tank, so we can use it round the farm and save a bit of money.

JENNY: What?

RYAN: It's totally safe. It's just something Pete came up with to help us out a bit.

JENNY: What the hell do you think you're doing?

RYAN: What?

JENNY: How could you do that without talking to me?

RYAN: Yeah, but the thing is, you can only really tap into it safely when the pipe's closed for cleaning. So Pete checked the cleaning rotas, and it was this weekend, and you were away visiting Grandma. So we had to go ahead while we could.

JENNY: That's completely irrelevant.

RYAN: No, it had to be now.

JENNY: It didn't have to happen at all, Ryan, what were you thinking?

PETE: It's very safe though, Jenny. Cos no one ever actually checks these pipes, unless something breaks. They just run a machine through when they need to clean it, it's robots, it's not people.

JENNY: It's not so much getting caught as doing it in the first place I'm questioning, Pete, I don't understand why you've done this.

RYAN: All right Mum, chill out.

JENNY: I want you to take it out.

RYAN: Why?

JENNY: You can't leave it like that, all right? Take it apart again.

PETE: That wouldn't be very easy, though.

JENNY: Why not?

PETE: I've made a massive hole in it now.

JENNY: So close it back up again.

RYAN: Mum, think about this for a minute. I'm sorry I didn't tell you in advance. But I knew you wouldn't be OK with it.

JENNY: Got that right.

RYAN: Come on Mum, don't be like this.

JENNY: D'you know what? I can't talk to you now, Ryan. I'm too tired to have a row, I don't want to start, all right? Lou, I'm going in.

LOU: OK.

JENNY: D'you want to come in with me?

LOU: All right.

JENNY: Thank you. Let's get away from this. I'm sorry Pete, I'd like to be more welcoming, but I'm a bit shocked, you understand?

PETE: I'm sorry if I've upset you, Jenny.

JENNY: It's not – Ryan, we'll talk about this in the morning, OK? We'll talk when you've calmed down. Come on love.

JENNY exits.

LOU: I'd better go after her.

RYAN: You don't have to.

LOU: No, but I better had.

LOU exits.

RYAN: Fuck's sake.

PETE: She'll be all right.

RYAN: Pisses me off.

PETE: You knew she'd be weird about it.

RYAN: At least I'm trying things. Why would you keep doing something that doesn't work? That's the definition of – I dunno, it's the definition of something fucking stupid.

RYAN tries not to cry.

PETE: You all right mate?

RYAN: I'm fine. Fuck it anyway. I'm so fucking glad you're back.

PETE: Yeah?

RYAN: Fucking band's back together, you know? Till tonight, we were sinking. I've felt like I was drowning this last year.

PETE: We won't let you go under mate. Fuck me, what's Hampshire for if it isn't for keeping you here and making the bread that feeds us? People like you go down, you take the whole thing with you. You're the anchor, Ryan. We're the links in the chain.

RYAN: I'm the anchor?

PETE: That's it.

RYAN: Yeah. Fucking right, man.

PETE: Your mum'll be all right. Lou'll talk her round.

RYAN: You think?

PETE: She'll talk her down, she gets it.

RYAN: I dunno, man.

PETE: What?

RYAN: It's not how it was for her.

PETE: How so?

RYAN: She's checked out a little bit. First week she was in the new job, they made an offer for the land.

PETE: Yeah?

15

RYAN: To build twenty new houses, all along here. Mum wouldn't look at it.

PETE: Good offer?

RYAN: Good enough. She said to me, you ever change your mind, you let me know. She wants different things to me these days. Is that why you've helped, is it Lou?

PETE: I'm just trying to help you.

RYAN: Yeah?

PETE: What?

RYAN: No agenda here mate. Mum'll have her hackles up about you.

PETE: Course.

RYAN: She thinks you're the antichrist.

PETE: That's just the way I do my hair.

They laugh.

PETE: It was good to see her, obviously.

RYAN: What, Mum?

PETE: Fuck off. Lou.

RYAN: D'you still feel like you – you know.

PETE: I was wondering whether she'd wanna go for a drink some time.

RYAN: Yeah?

PETE: I dunno whether she'd be up for it though.

RYAN: We don't really talk about stuff like that.

PETE: No, course. Anyway. I've got a new job lined up.

RYAN: Serious?

PETE: Yeah.

RYAN: What?

PETE: Just oil stuff. Good gig.

RYAN: Oh, I'm so fucking glad, mate. Fuck. I'm so happy there's work for you again.

PETE: Yeah.

RYAN: I know I've said it before, but I've been so cut up, what happened. I know I didn't do my bit.

PETE: It's not like that. Don't think like that.

RYAN: But when I got off, ever since I got off. I know I was lucky. And I'm so sorry about that. And I'm so fucking glad that you can move on from it. I thought you'd never speak to me again.

PETE: Why?

RYAN: Thought I wouldn't deserve to be mates with you anymore. It was nothing to do with you, you know. When Lou stopped visiting.

PETE: I get it.

RYAN: Bag searches, and. I mean it was stressful enough for me when I went in, you know? For Lou, going in there to see her boyfriend, that's heavy, innit.

PETE: Exactly.

RYAN: It was just more than she could handle after Dad.

PETE: Right. Just as hard for her as it is for you, innit.

RYAN: Course.

PETE: And your mum and all.

RYAN: Course.

PETE: Still only yesterday really, wasn't it.

RYAN: No.

PETE: No?

RYAN: It doesn't feel like it was yesterday. It feels like it's now. It feels like we're still losing him now. Like even as we speak, someone is cutting into me. I reckon she'd go for a drink with you.

PETE: Yeah?

RYAN: Be good if she wasn't on her own all the time.

PETE: Is she?

RYAN: Well, she goes to work, obviously. But then when she's home in the evenings, that's it. Be good if she got the odd break from Bereavement Island.

PETE: It is a bit like an island.

RYAN: Desolate and hostile.

PETE: But Bear Grylls never turns up and takes you home.

RYAN: No, the cunt, he doesn't.

PETE: She hasn't been seeing anyone else then?

RYAN: No, she wanted to be on her own.

PETE: Do you ever go out?

RYAN: How d'you mean?

PETE: You're saying Lou doesn't go anywhere. Do you?

RYAN: Well, I see you.

PETE: We've had what, three drinks in the last two months?

RYAN: I don't wanna see anyone else though.

PETE: Why not?

RYAN: I know this sounds stupid. But you went away while he was still here. So you weren't here when all of it happened. When I see you, it's like I've gone back to the old time. It's like you're still back there, and I can go back there too.

With everyone else, they know what he looked like when he had to wear the wig. They know how the story ended, you're still in the good bit of the book.

PETE: Right.

RYAN: I sound mental don't I.

PETE: No.

RYAN: Maybe a drink with you, maybe Lou'd like that.

PETE: Might feel the same for her. Like it didn't happen.

RYAN: Yeah.

PETE: You should try and see other people. Gotta try and stay socialised, gotta try and get out.

RYAN: I always thought you'd end up married.

PETE: Me and Lou?

RYAN: Yeah. Stupid, I just thought that'd be what happened.

PETE: One step at a time, maybe. Would you mind?

RYAN: If you two got married?

PETE: And we were like, proper brothers?

RYAN: We've been brothers for years, mate.

PETE: Yeah?

RYAN: Course we have. That's what this is about tonight. This is the kind of shit family do for each other.

JENNY: *(Off.)* Ryan!

RYAN: I'd better go.

JENNY: *(Off.)* Ryan!

PETE: Yeah man.

RYAN: Shall I bring out your clothes? I don't reckon you wanna try going in there tonight.

PETE: No, you're all right.

JENNY: *(Off.)* Ryan!

RYAN: Speak later yeah?

PETE: Yeah, man. All right.

RYAN picks up his clothes and exits. PETE starts to get dressed again, watching the stars wheel all around him as the lights go down.

SCENE TWO

The following evening. Night will fall across the course of the scene. A patio space at the front of the farmhouse. A picnic table. There's an old metal bin on the edge of the patio. RYAN is hefting a rifle. He aims at a crow settling on a line, and shoots. He exits in the direction he fired in. JENNY enters with a pile of envelopes, a portable speaker, a string of fairy lights and a glass of wine. RYAN enters, gun in one hand, dead crow hanging from the other.

RYAN: One for the pot.

JENNY: Don't be disgusting.

RYAN: Goes to waste otherwise.

JENNY: You couldn't eat a crow.

RYAN: Why not?

JENNY sits down to open her post with a glass of wine.

JENNY: It's a criminal offence to shoot them, for one thing.

RYAN: It's not.

JENNY: It is.

RYAN: They eat the ducklings. They've had three already.

He drops the crow to the floor.

JENNY: Don't just dump it!

RYAN: Why's it a crime to shoot crows?

JENNY: It's an offence to shoot any wild birds.

RYAN: No way.

JENNY: You should know that.

RYAN: I knew it was a crime when those homeless blokes in Windsor ate swans.

JENNY: That doesn't happen does it?

RYAN: Didn't know it was all birds.

JENNY: Well. People like to say these days that everyone poor is a victim, but a thing like that reminds you.

RYAN: Thing like what?

JENNY: Let's just say I'd have to stoop very low indeed before I thought about eating a swan. I think that says a lot about a person's character.

RYAN: Well, maybe if you were hungry.

JENNY: They're a symbol of our queen.

RYAN: She might want us to eat if we were hungry.

JENNY: Oh, I can't talk about it, I get so patriotic.

RYAN: That bill's got red on it.

JENNY: Thank you Ryan, I'm not actually colourblind.

RYAN: All OK?

JENNY: Fine, don't worry.

RYAN: Doesn't have to be so scary with a bit of extra coming in. *(He gestures to the pipe.)*

JENNY: I am not spending money from that on proper bills.

RYAN: Why not?

JENNY: I'm not gonna condone it, Ryan.

RYAN: So cos it's naughty money we can only use it to buy naughty things?

JENNY: I don't want it used at all, Ryan, I want it disconnected.

RYAN: All right, just saying. If you ever wanted me to help out with the books –

JENNY: I was all right looking after them while your dad was around. I don't think they've got too much more complicated now.

RYAN: But you never did all of it. Dad was –

JENNY: This is my bit, Ryan. This is how I can contribute, you have your way you contribute. Let me have my bit.

RYAN: But we're all right, are we? We can pay that bill?

JENNY: This bill isn't Britain's most important document, it's the bloody internet or something, the phones, I don't know, it's not a big deal. Yes, I can and will pay it.

RYAN: All right.

JENNY: Everything's under control.

RYAN: All right

JENNY: Are you home now? I want to talk to you.

RYAN: Sure.

JENNY: I'm sorry I was upset last night. I shouldn't have let myself – well we don't get anywhere being emotional, do we. Nice to see Pete again.

RYAN: Yeah?

JENNY: Quite a surprise. Is he all right? Is he living at his mum's?

RYAN: Yeah.

JENNY: And what about work?

RYAN: He's got his old job back.

JENNY: Oh right?

RYAN: They've told him so, he told me last night. Took a while, but. Takes years to train a welder, doesn't it, costs a lot. So you don't just chuck 'em out because they lamp someone. They were never gonna just chuck him out. It's all tough boys down Fawley, they've had blokes go to prison before.

JENNY: I bet.

RYAN: They let him back doing contract work straight off.

JENNY: So he's been working?

RYAN: Yeah.

JENNY: And this was something he's persuaded you would be a good idea, this thing you've done, that right?

RYAN: Not really. We decided on it together.

JENNY: Right. And are you going to take it apart again?

RYAN: Why would I?

JENNY: What would your father have thought of a grubby little scam like that? He'd have nothing to do with it.

RYAN: That whole tank's full up. Think what we'll save. The heat. The light. The engines. And then if we skim any excess we can sell it. It's like a new crop.

JENNY: It's hardly a crop.

RYAN: You want a new car, don't you?

JENNY: Yes.

RYAN: So this will buy us a new car.

JENNY: Criminal proceeds though, isn't it? What's next? Brothel in the grain store?

RYAN: Brothels aren't illegal, I don't think.

JENNY: Actually they are, it's prostitution's fine, which is a complete mess, but let's not go into it. If it didn't feel so underhand I'd be fine, Ryan, I like new handbags as much as the next girl, but I want this farm to be run as your dad would have wanted, and I don't think he would have wanted that.

RYAN: Well the holes are made now, aren't they, damage is done. People would still know what we'd done, even if we took it apart again.

JENNY: Right.

RYAN: I'm sorry, but it's done.

JENNY: D'you want a glass of wine?

RYAN: I'm trying not to drink in the week, actually.

JENNY: Are you?

RYAN: Yeah.

JENNY: Really?

RYAN: Yes.

JENNY: You?

RYAN: All right.

JENNY: What's brought this on, who are you dating?

RYAN: No, it's the early mornings, that's all.

JENNY: Oh right.

RYAN: That all right with you?

JENNY: You're definitely dating.

RYAN: Mum.

JENNY: Fair enough. Just give me notice if she's coming round for dinner. And I'll need to buy some ear plugs if she's going to stay the night.

RYAN: Hilarious.

JENNY: What's going on between him and Lou?

RYAN: Speaking of noisy sex, is that the connection you just made?

JENNY: Ryan. What's the story? Have they talked? They haven't been meeting up?

RYAN: No.

JENNY: Where are they at with each other?

RYAN: I dunno.

Another crow circles towards the wire.

RYAN: Here you come, you bastard.

RYAN takes aim with the gun.

JENNY: Your father shot a Labrador here once.

RYAN: Seriously?

RYAN shoots. He misses.

RYAN: Bollocks.

JENNY: There was this old boy who'd retired down here. I think he wanted to be nearer the fishing. And he had a great fat black lab, big fat dog, I don't know what he fed it, he walked it enough, but it was enormous. And he used to walk it right across this lawn, right there.

RYAN: Joking.

JENNY: Before Dad did it up, when it was still just a scrap of field. Used it as a cut through, see, saved crossing the river. But of course it wasn't a right of way.

RYAN: No.

JENNY: So Des said to him one day, I don't know the hundredth time this bloke came trampling through, and he was having a hard day I think, your dad, or anyway he was in a foul mood, is the salient point, and he said if that dog crosses my land again I'm going to shoot it.

RYAN: Ha!

JENNY: I think it must have relieved itself against the hedge or something, but whatever the reason, he took against it. Now evidently, the gentleman who owned the dog didn't take Dad at his word. And a few days later, Dad spotted him making his way toward the field again. So he got the gun, and went up to our bedroom and settled in the window. And when the dog stepped onto the field, he got it in the neck.

RYAN: Amazing.

JENNY: Stone dead. He was a good shot.

RYAN: What did the guy do?

JENNY: Well, I don't know exactly, I wasn't there myself. But eventually I know he carried the dog off home back the way he came. Carried it in his arms, like that. Bet he regretted the weight of it then. He moved away not long after, and good riddance to bad rubbish I say, thinking the whole country's there to be walked all over by people who've come down from town.

RYAN: Amazing.

JENNY: I was cross with your dad at the time, but you do see the funny side all these years later. Are you going to get rid of that crow?

RYAN: I thought I'd string it up somewhere as a warning.

JENNY: A warning to who?

RYAN: Other crows.

JENNY: Will that work?

RYAN: It might. They're scared of scarecrows aren't they. So imagine how freaked they'll be when they circle over and see one of their dead mates hanging off the washing line.

JENNY: I don't really want dead animals hanging all round the house, Ryan. Bit *Blair Witch*.

RYAN: Suit yourself.

RYAN picks up the crow and lobs it offstage.

JENNY: Would we count that as adequate corpse disposal?

RYAN: It'll do for now, won't it? I can't be arsed burying it. Fox'll sort it out, he'll think that's delicious.

JENNY: You could put it in the bin.

RYAN: I'll do it later.

JENNY: He wants to get back with her, of course. Does he know? You know, about –

RYAN: No.

JENNY: I think she's outgrown him.

RYAN: On what evidence?

JENNY: Well, we talk every day, I do talk to her.

RYAN: What does she say makes you think that?

JENNY: It's nothing specific, it's not like that. I just have this feeling.

RYAN: Right.

JENNY sees another crow.

JENNY: Give me that.

RYAN gives her the gun. She hunches down to aim.

JENNY: I am her mother. Mothers have their intuition.

JENNY shoots. A crow falls dead onto the stage.

RYAN: Shot.

JENNY: Thank you.

JENNY goes to the crow, picks it up as RYAN speaks to her. She looks around for somewhere to put it, crosses to the bin, drops the crow in, giving RYAN the eye as she does so.

RYAN: It won't work you know, Mum.

JENNY: What?

RYAN: You can't just talk her out of whatever she's feeling. It doesn't work like that. If you go on about him you'll only piss her off, and then you're just pushing her towards him. So it won't even work, whether or not it's the right thing to do in the first place.

JENNY: I know I get too involved sometimes. It's only because I care. I know I make you angry.

RYAN: No.

JENNY: Anyone would get frustrated having to be always round their mum. God knows, it's a miracle I never killed Grandma. I'm never all right, that's the trouble.

RYAN: I know.

JENNY: It's natural to miss him. And we didn't get as long as we deserved with him, did we. You're the spit of how he looked when we first met. When I was still living at home, and he got me to move out here. He used to drive over in his car, I'd hear the radio playing while I was coming down the stairs. Sometimes I feel like I'd love to be greedy and spend a whole evening remembering him. I like to imagine if I got into bed with a pint of wine, and you and Lou sat on the bed with me, and we got out every photo anyone ever took with him in it, and laid them all out on the bed, and told each other every story we could think of with him in it till the dawn broke, or the owls were swooping, and we couldn't keep our eyes open any more, then fell asleep together you two next to me in bed like when you were little. But it never happens, a thing like that, does it.

RYAN: No.

JENNY: We're never all together somehow.

RYAN: No.

JENNY: I like to pretend he can hear me.

RYAN: Yeah?

JENNY: I like to think he's with me all the day. Even when he was alive, I used to do that. I liked things more if I imagined what he'd think of them. It was more like sharing my life.

RYAN: And you do that now?

JENNY: In my head, I talk to him about everything. In my head I'm with him now.

The sound of a car.

JENNY: That'll be Lou. Put the gun down, Ryan.

RYAN puts the gun down. Enter LOU.

LOU: Hiya.

JENNY: Hello my love. You're late back.

LOU: Am I? Sorry. I got some wine in.

JENNY: Lovely. I'll get it in the fridge shall I?

RYAN: You all right?

JENNY: Yeah. Be out in a minute.

JENNY exits.

LOU: She all right?

RYAN: We were just talking about Dad. Think she got a bit.

LOU: Oh yeah.

RYAN: Did you know he shot a Labrador out that window?

LOU: Oh, yeah. Mental.

RYAN: Did you know that story?

LOU: Dad told me. Mum kicked him out for a week after that.

RYAN: Really?

LOU: She thought he'd get us all arrested. Shouting and screaming, don't you remember?

RYAN: God. You all right?

LOU: I'm OK. Sometimes I feel really anxious when I'm coming up that drive.

RYAN: Yeah?

LOU: I dunno. Driving home sometimes, I get all jumpy like the sky's falling in.

RYAN: Well it's back in the cage again, isn't it.

JENNY enters with two more glasses of wine.

JENNY: Here's one cold already!

RYAN: Nice one Mum.

LOU: Thanks so much.

JENNY: There we go. So, darling, how are you, good day?

LOU: Yeah, all right.

JENNY: Good. Nice wine, this, isn't it.

LOU: Yeah.

JENNY: I used to be more of a chardonnay drinker but it's not so much the fashion any more. Course you won't remember

Footballer's Wives, too young. I think I'm quite influenced in my tastes by cookery programmes, you know.

LOU: Yeah?

JENNY: And what's on the shelves. God knows what I actually like best myself, I think a lot of the time I'm just cooking and drinking what people recommend on the telly. *Saturday Kitchen*'s very good for wines, I watch it on catchup sometimes when I can't sleep. Not as good now it's not James Martin. I don't know what my favourite sort of wine actually is. Do you two?

LOU: No, not really. Better white than red maybe.

JENNY: Yeah.

LOU: Is that chicken eating that crow's eyes?

RYAN: Oh, shit.

RYAN throws a stone.

JENNY: I told you to put that away.

LOU: That's dark.

RYAN: Juicy place to start. I'll just –

RYAN exits.

JENNY: Oh, I know what I wanted to do.

JENNY picks up the long string of fairy lights. She plugs them into the wall of the house and starts to string them over the stage.

LOU: They're nice.

JENNY: I thought I'd try and spruce it up, since we're spending so much time out here this summer.

LOU: Yeah, lovely. Wanna hand?

JENNY: Go on then.

LOU helps JENNY put up the fairy lights.

LOU: Where are we going with them?

JENNY: I just think sort of get 'em up in the air, you know? So you must have had Pete on your mind all day.

LOU: A bit, yeah.

JENNY: Shaken you up?

LOU: Well I was happy to see him as well.

JENNY: Yeah, sure.

LOU: Ryan tell you he might pop round tonight?

JENNY: No?

LOU: Aftercare, basically. Check there's nothing wrong with the job over there.

JENNY: Will you see him then, if he comes over?

LOU: I dunno. I don't feel like I need to hide away from him. I don't particularly feel like I need to talk to him either. Yesterday it was all right. I was scared at first, but we said hi. Then we hardly talked, they were busy. They'll be busy again tonight.

JENNY: Right. Isn't that beautiful?

LOU: Lovely.

They admire the fairy lights.

JENNY: And, check this out.

JENNY takes out her phone and fiddles with it.

LOU: Have you just discovered it's got the internet?

JENNY: No, sarky. Listen to this.

JENNY presses a button on her phone, and music starts to play from the table. Sting's 'La Belle Dame Sans Regrets'.

LOU: That's cool.

JENNY: Look.

JENNY goes to the table and picks up a set of wireless speakers.

JENNY: Weatherproof. I thought we could hang them out here, long as summer lasts.

LOU: Cool.

JENNY: Only thirty quid. Ryan'll say we should have spent it on something sensible but I thought if we're gonna save all this cash on fuel, I'll buy whatever the hell I want, so I got 'em in town this afternoon at the same time as I was getting all nice things in for tea. I never know the words to this one. Not good enough at French. What shall we listen to?

LOU: You choose.

JENNY: Well me and your dad always liked Fleetwood Mac.

LOU: All right, *Rumours* then.

JENNY: They've got other albums.

LOU: Yeah, but we're gonna listen to *Rumours*.

JENNY: Favourite song?

LOU: I dunno.

JENNY: I know what I like.

JENNY searches on her phone. 'Never Going Back Again' starts to play. JENNY dances along to it.

LOU: Such a hippy.

JENNY: You could join in.

LOU: I'm not joining in.

JENNY: Come on.

LOU: No way.

JENNY starts singing. After the first two lines, LOU joins in with the singing. JENNY keeps dancing. Before the second verse, she stops the song.

JENNY: That's enough of that.

LOU: I was enjoying that.

JENNY: Enjoying me making a fool of myself.

LOU: You were quite good.

JENNY: Silly old woman dancing, I feel all shy now.

LOU: Why, who can see us to care? Good song, innit.

JENNY: We saw them live once. Long ago.

LOU: Pete took me to see them at the O2.

JENNY: Course he did, I'd forgotten that. Well he's not all bad then, is he.

LOU: I'll do these.

LOU starts on the candles.

JENNY: Why've you got a lighter? You're not smoking?

LOU: No. They're just useful.

JENNY: Oh right.

LOU: Only a menthol after work, never killed anyone.

JENNY: I think it probably did.

LOU: I'll quit in a bit. Just a bit stressed at the moment. Work and whatever.

JENNY: They work you too hard, I think.

LOU: I'm fine. We should all stop treating each other like we're made of glass. Then maybe we wouldn't feel as fragile. I wanted to talk to you about something.

JENNY: Yes?

LOU: An idea.

JENNY: Go on.

LOU: When I move out again, I was thinking you ought to do Airbnb with my room.

JENNY: Are you thinking of moving back out?

LOU: I know last time I moved out you kept my room.

JENNY: Turned out to be good that we did.

LOU: Yeah. But I don't think you should feel you have to do that any more. When I move out next, I mean.

JENNY: Because you won't be coming home again.

LOU: I'll be making a new home.

JENNY: I don't want you to move back out.

LOU: I know. But.

JENNY: What?

LOU: We could have flown the nest a bit more than we have, I think. People are meant to go their own way, aren't they.

JENNY: That's Fleetwood Mac as well.

LOU: God it is, isn't it.

JENNY: All the time we think we're speaking for ourselves and we're only quoting lyrics. Isn't it weird? Imagine how much of our heads is made up out of other people thinking. I won't be living here for ever myself, of course.

LOU: No?

JENNY: Well. If Ryan does ever manage to lure someone back here, I guess I'd have to go.

LOU: Do you sometimes think it'd be good for you to go anyway?

JENNY: Of course not.

LOU: No, sure.

JENNY: I thought about turning the back bedroom into a granny flat, you know, Ryan's bedroom. You could build stairs up the back of the house maybe. But I haven't said anything to Ryan. I know he'd say no, and I can't really bear it. Having to go one day. And I wouldn't want to change the house, I like it how it is. I don't really know what I'm going to do if he ever meets someone.

LOU: We ought to give some thought to it all.

RYAN enters.

RYAN: Sorted. And I got the chickens in. That my glass?

LOU: Yeah.

RYAN sits down with the others on the picnic bench.

JENNY: Thought you weren't having any?

RYAN: Just a glass maybe. I hear music?

JENNY: Oh, yeah. I got some speakers.

RYAN: Cool. Put something on then.

JENNY: Oh yeah, sorry.

JENNY busies herself with her phone.

RYAN: Nice evening. That's probably Mars, look, winking at us.

LOU: Why are you shooting crows?

RYAN: Keep 'em off the ducklings.

LOU: Have the ducklings hatched?

RYAN: Yeah. Course, you haven't seen 'em, you've been out all day. They'll be asleep now. Have a look in the morning, they're cute.

Everything But The Girl's 'Amplified Heart' starts playing.

LOU: The music you like is all older than us.

JENNY: You wait and see, the world will leave you behind as well before you know it.

RYAN: We'll be in the hospice singing Eminem.

JENNY: Would you rather we listened to him?

RYAN: Don't think it's the right vibe really Mum.

JENNY: OK. Lou's been telling me she's feeling a bit funny about Pete.

LOU: Mum.

RYAN: Oh right.

JENNY: I was just saying, wasn't I, how tricky it must feel for you.

RYAN: Probably something to talk about with Pete, not us, don't you think?

JENNY: Ryan.

LOU: What do you mean?

RYAN: Just saying.

LOU: I was just chatting to Mum.

RYAN: I'm just saying.

LOU: It helps me to talk things through.

RYAN: But maybe more with Pete than Mum and me though, Lou.

LOU: I haven't talked to Pete in half a year though, have I. It's not a simple thing to start again.

JENNY: I worry about how happy he can make you.

RYAN: Mum.

JENNY: What?

LOU: Why d'you say that?

JENNY: Well you've been brought up a certain way, haven't you. And people get used to a certain way of things working. And you've been brought up into one world, all your life, and people around you, and things like that. Pete's not like that, is he. He's not close to his family. He doesn't understand our work. He does that job because it's how he can make money, he's got no feeling, not like we have a feeling for this. He's got us filling that septic tank with that muck. Because all he sees there is money, not everything else it means. I don't think he could imagine for a moment why we do what we do. And try to be a family. And look after things, so we can pass them on.

RYAN: I'd swap with him.

JENNY: No you wouldn't.

RYAN: If I got the chance. If I could have what he has, I'd take it, course I would. Modern house you can actually keep warm. Days off.

JENNY: And a year in prison and a record following him round for ever?

RYAN: That's done, that's behind him.

JENNY: You put some poor lad in a wheelchair, you can't just put it behind you. He'll be in that chair for ever.

RYAN: He fell and hit his head on a kerb. That wasn't us, not really.

JENNY: The boy you were would never have got involved. He changed you.

RYAN: Did he.

JENNY: Already had a record, that was already who he was.

RYAN: He got suspended from school, he didn't have a record.

JENNY: Adds up the same. Your Dad worked his whole life to give all this to you, how could you say you'd rather be down there? You'd just rather be away from me.

LOU: Mum, don't pick a fight, all right?

JENNY: I'm sorry. But I think that's crap, frankly, Ryan, I think you're just trying to upset me. I don't know how I'm supposed to hold us together when you talk like that. We were all right, us three. This is what happens when other people get involved. That is all of his lack of respect for anything right there, smirking at me. Flooding your Dad's farm, drowning. He comes from a different world, can you see that? He comes from a different world, and it will infect us, it'll make us sick.

RYAN: What are you talking about?

JENNY: That muck, that sludge, don't you see it?

RYAN: Why's it any dirtier what he does than me or Lou?

JENNY: Drilling for oil?

RYAN: I chuck chemicals on wheat, Mum. I chuck chemicals all round the place and I operate machinery. The idea that farming is some old pure fucking way of life is dead, if it ever even existed. I'm not a treehugger, I'm not a lentil eater, I make money, I make food. We're not druids living off roots, so don't act like you're better than him.

LOU: I don't think we were all right.

JENNY: What?

LOU: The three of us. Don't say we're all right without Pete, we're not. I did love him, Mum.

The sound of a car.

JENNY: That's him, isn't it.

LOU: Yeah.

JENNY: Oh, great.

LOU: It's all right, he's just come to check on the pipe.

Enter PETE.

PETE: Hi.

RYAN: All right mate?

PETE: Yeah, getting there. How are you Jenny?

JENNY: Fine, thank you for asking. How are you Pete?

PETE: Great. All right?

LOU: All right.

JENNY: You come to catch up about yesterday?

PETE: That's it, yeah.

JENNY: And we can catch up with you.

PETE: Yeah.

JENNY: Great. Does anyone want some wine and some nibbles maybe? I've got these cheesy things in the fridge.

PETE: Yeah. All right, thanks, yeah.

JENNY: Hang on. Let me bring a bottle out.

JENNY exits.

PETE: How is it then? I'm assuming we're OK, or you'd have called me.

RYAN: Yeah, man, it's good.

PETE: Working OK?

RYAN: I tried opening and closing the tap this morning, all good.

PETE: All right. So it sounds like we're all right then.

RYAN: It's working like a dream mate, all good.

PETE: OK. Cool.

RYAN: You wanna see it?

PETE: Yeah, erm, yeah in a bit.

RYAN: Sure, yeah, sorry.

Enter JENNY with wine and nibbles.

JENNY: Here we go then. Let's all take the weight off?

RYAN: All right?

JENNY: You sit with me, Lou.

They all sit down together.

JENNY: These are meant to be good I think.

RYAN has eaten one.

RYAN: Nice, yeah.

JENNY: Good. Want one?

LOU: Ta.

JENNY: Remember when we had that fruit salad here, Pete, and you ended up in the hospital?

PETE: Yeah.

JENNY: Your face.

PETE: Swelled right up, yeah.

JENNY: I still can't imagine what I put in there that did it.

RYAN: We thought it was probably the handle on Dad's chainsaw, wasn't it?

JENNY: Did we?

RYAN: Cos he'd left it on the kitchen table.

JENNY: Oh yeah. Anyway, your face.

PETE: You took that photo of me while I was in the hospital.

JENNY: I know. I knew we'd laugh about it later.

PETE: Yeah.

JENNY: I could go and find it if you like?

RYAN: Maybe later Mum.

JENNY: Sure, yeah. Anyway, look. I don't want to get dramatic or whatever, but I feel like I ought to say it's great to see you, Pete. I'm sure I speak for us all when I say that it's great to see you again.

PETE: Thank you.

JENNY: Because you were like a part of this family, weren't you. And that's been terrible, when we were so used to seeing you all the time, not to see you at all.

RYAN: Yeah.

JENNY: Though of course I know Ryan's been meeting up with you since you got out, I know. But you see what I mean.

PETE: Of course.

JENNY: And I don't want to get upset, but I think I should probably say, I hope I didn't come across as hostile when I saw you last night. I don't want to be hostile to you.

LOU: It's all right, Mum.

JENNY: Sorry. I just want to – it's very upsetting, something like that happening behind your back, and I do feel quite juddered by it. I won't deny that. But we ought to try to separate out the different things going on here now, you know? Because I can still be upset about that, and pleased to see you back here, can't I.

PETE: Sure.

JENNY: Good. Good. So I think that was all that I wanted to say. I don't want to make a big speech or anything. I just wanted to say, Ryan and I do need to work through the implications of what happened last night, it's not something I'm very satisfied with right now, but I don't want that to get in the way of welcoming you back onto the farm.

RYAN: Hear hear.

PETE: I really appreciate that Jenny, thank you.

JENNY: Really –

PETE: And I did want to apologise to you tonight as well.

JENNY: Oh right.

PETE: I hope you'll see all I wanted to do was help out my friend. And be a good friend. And do you a favour as well, of course. But I understand, having thought about last night, and you coming home last night like you did, I understand that it will have been a shock, and I'm sorry about that.

JENNY: Well I appreciate that.

PETE: I do think it's a good idea, what we've done, I should say that too. I do think it's smart. But of course I wouldn't have wanted to meet you again like that.

JENNY: And me, Pete. I didn't want to snap.

PETE: All right. Well I'm sorry then.

JENNY: Thank you.

PETE: These are good, aren't they.

JENNY: M and S. Get what you pay for, don't you.

RYAN: Got any more?

JENNY: I think there's another packet inside, shall I get them?

LOU: Yeah, please, Mum.

JENNY: All right. We all right for drinks?

LOU: All right.

JENNY: One sec.

JENNY exits.

LOU: I thought you two were gonna start making out in a minute.

PETE: I'm just trying to be straight with her.

LOU: Bit weird.

PETE: Well it's a weird situation, isn't it.

Music starts playing, very loudly – George Michael, 'Faith'.

PETE: Fuck me.

Enter JENNY.

JENNY: Whaddaya think of these, Pete?

PETE: Erm –

JENNY: Bluetooth speakers. Just got 'em. Cool right? I thought we could get some tunes going.

RYAN: Bit loud, Mum.

JENNY: All right, all right.

She turns the music down a bit.

JENNY: Couldn't tell the balance from inside, you know? You can operate it from your phone. Here we go, I got dips as well, and Doritos.

RYAN: Nice.

JENNY: Well then. This is nice, isn't it. This is nice.

RYAN: It's good to be able to sit outside, isn't it. Enjoy an evening.

LOU: Yeah.

JENNY: Dad loved evenings like this. All of us together, and you used to come over, and we'd all sit outside and drink.

PETE: Yeah.

JENNY: Of course that will have been the last you saw of him, won't it. After the trial, that was the last time you saw each other.

PETE: Yeah.

JENNY: Bloody hell. Isn't that amazing? All that time in between disappears, when you think of it like that.

PETE: I guess so, yeah.

JENNY: Bloody hell. I wish it would. You know we would all have liked to visit more.

PETE: I know.

RYAN: We've done this Mum.

JENNY: All right.

PETE: It's all good.

JENNY: All right.

PETE: I would have liked to have been there for you guys as well, you know. I'm sorry.

JENNY: We thought of you at the funeral. We did think of you, wished you were there.

PETE: I was there in spirit.

LOU starts to cry.

RYAN: All right mate, all right.

RYAN puts an arm around her shoulders. JENNY turns off the music.

LOU: Sorry.

RYAN: It's all right.

LOU: I'm sorry. I don't wanna cry every time, I know it's not – what a shit year though, was 2016. Fucking Prince. David Bowie. Professor Snape. Willie Wonka. George Michael. Dad.

RYAN: Yeah.

LOU: I wish no one else had died except for him.

JENNY: Why?

LOU: So people wouldn't forget about him.

JENNY: No one's going to forget your dad.

LOU: You wait. Ten years' time, people will say, 2016, that was the year all the pop stars were dying. Terry Wogan and Muhammad Ali. You wait and see. And we'll have to smile and nod and we won't know how to tell them, that didn't matter. That didn't matter at all.

JENNY: It's all right my love.

LOU: Sorry. I can't stand it. People think the most important thing in the world's some fucking referendum. Why won't anyone notice? Why won't anyone notice that doesn't matter at all?

JENNY: Yeah.

RYAN: The people who matter will always know, won't they. Our people. Us four here.

LOU: Yeah.

RYAN: And we don't need anyone else.

LOU: Maybe, yeah.

JENNY: We have to make sure that we remember him, that's all. We have to keep that much of him alive. And set the example to people, and be the example. We have to remember what it used to be like, here, when he was here, and fight to keep things as he would have wanted.

LOU: Do we?

JENNY: That'll be his legacy. All this.

LOU: Just a few fields, is that it?

JENNY: That's not what it is, love. It's more than that.

LOU: I dunno. I'm sorry, I dunno.

RYAN: You're all right.

LOU: I know.

RYAN: You don't have to be sad, then.

LOU: I'm sorry. It's just too weird, having him here.

RYAN: Oh.

LOU: I'm sorry, I can't – it's too weird to just pretend that it doesn't feel frightening you being here with us. It's making me upset.

PETE: I'm sorry.

LOU: I'm not having a go. I just can't play along, like.

PETE: Do you want me to go?

LOU: No, I just – I don't want to sit here pretending to be happy. Being civil, I don't want that.

JENNY: Lou, love.

PETE: I can go if that's easiest.

LOU: No, I don't want you to. I just don't wanna make nice with Doritos. I don't see the point in pretending the world is a nice and normal place where people have snacks, when it's not, when it's fucking evil.

JENNY: Darling.

LOU: You can't just take it away hanging up a few fairy lights, can you. It doesn't work like that.

JENNY: All right. I'm sorry.

RYAN: Maybe we ought to let you have a bit of a chat then, if you're feeling –

LOU: I don't wanna chase everyone away.

RYAN: Yeah, but maybe if you're feeling like that. Mum?

JENNY: Yeah?

RYAN: What if we go in and cook, what d'you think?

JENNY: I don't want you to feel on your own, Lou. I want you to know that you're never on your own, all right? I'm always here, I'm always with you.

LOU: Yeah. I know.

RYAN: Why don't we let you have a moment, the both of you?

LOU: Yeah, maybe.

RYAN: And you can tell Pete whatever you want to tell him.

JENNY: Ryan.

RYAN: I'm just saying. Maybe we give them a minute out here. Why don't we go in and start on the food?

JENNY: You all right if I go in?

LOU: Yeah.

JENNY: OK. You just call if you need me then, all right?

LOU: Yeah.

JENNY: You all right Pete?

PETE: I'm fine, yeah. I'm sorry, I didn't mean to –

RYAN: You're all right mate. Come on Mum.

JENNY: I'll just be inside love, all right?

LOU: All right.

JENNY: Just call if you need me.

LOU: Yeah.

JENNY and RYAN exit.

PETE: Long time since it was just the two of us talking.

LOU: Yeah.

PETE: You all right?

LOU: No. I'm all right.

PETE: Beautiful out here. Gets good and dark. Never dark over the plant. Not so you see a sky like this one. Funny really.

LOU: What?

PETE: I spend all day drowned in steel and lights. I used to look at films of refineries in school. I'd never have guessed till I worked there all the people who keep them running come home to places like these. From a distance it looks like the moon. But when I'm working down by the water I'm watching seals bob up in the bay. And we come home and we're here, we're wild. You'd never think we lived in both worlds just from watching the documentaries. Don't you wanna talk to me?

LOU: I don't know what to say.

PETE: You don't have to say anything big, I'd just love to talk to you.

LOU: Well we are, aren't we?

PETE: Yeah. I've missed you.

LOU: Yeah.

PETE: I got too used to telling you everything. Haven't had anyone to talk to when I'm worried about stuff for too long.

LOU: Must have been hard.

PETE: It's all right. Just kept my head down. Through it all now anyway. Looking better now. I've got a new job lined up.

LOU: That's good.

PETE: They want to send me to Dubai.

LOU: Oh right.

PETE: So I'll get it all back, Lou. The things we were working towards, they're not lost. I didn't miss my chance, it's just been – on hold for a bit. And now I can get back to it. It'll be like all that never happened.

LOU: That'll be nice for you.

PETE: I'm sorry. I didn't mean to say the wrong thing.

LOU: No, you're fine.

PETE: You got a new job as well. Ryan was telling me.

LOU: Yeah.

PETE: Tell me about it then?

LOU: Well, it's just an admin job for a construction company. They build houses. We did the big new development over Fair Oak, you know?

PETE: I drive past it, yeah.

LOU: Loads of it round here now, everywhere. We buy land off of farmers, round the edge of the towns, and expand the towns out. They tried to buy this.

PETE: I heard.

LOU: Mum was spitting. I try and tell her we do good work. People need homes. We look after people really. She doesn't buy it of course.

PETE: You enjoy it?

LOU: I just wanted a reason to get out the house. First place I heard about a vacancy when I started looking. People used to be defined by their work, I think. They made that who they were. We couldn't do that now even if we wanted to, our generation. Where's the job secure enough to offer that?

PETE: Right.

LOU: And I think we know it's a swizz.

PETE: Yeah?

LOU: People used to only see their bit of the world. We can get on a plane and go somewhere. We can google anywhere. So why make your life about your work? You're alive now, aren't you. That's the only bit we know we're gonna have. I used to feel like I was waiting for something. There used to be a future. Now there isn't any more somehow, it's now instead, I'm in it. And there's nothing much to it. So I just have to do what I can to make it better. And better pretty much meant getting out the house.

PETE: Right. Ryan was saying you're not out that much though.

LOU: Did he?

PETE: Maybe I could take you out some time? If you wanted to go somewhere?

LOU: I dunno whether I can be with someone at the moment.

PETE: Weren't we happy?

LOU: Lot's changed hasn't it.

PETE: I just wondered whether you'd go for a drink with me?

LOU: I dunno.

PETE: Really?

LOU: I can't decide, I feel –

PETE: It's OK. I don't mean to put pressure on you, I'm sorry.

LOU: You're all right.

PETE: Your mum doesn't want us together again.

LOU: She thinks you're the ghost of Christmas future.

PETE: How d'you mean?

LOU: Well it so nearly happened to Ryan, going down. And obviously she thinks about that when she thinks about you.

PETE: It's not gonna happen. Des had just had his diagnosis, we were ten pints in, Ryan was mental, it was a weird night.

LOU: You know what I mean though.

PETE: Come for a drink with me one time. We could go somewhere nice, we could go to the Black Boy.

LOU: Why do we have to talk about this now?

PETE: Cos I'm going away, Lou. They'll move me so far away from here, and I don't wanna just give up on you.

LOU: Why would I spend time with you if you're going away? I'll just get hurt some more.

PETE: I never wanted to hurt you.

LOU: Why've you waited so long to come and see me?

PETE: I didn't know whether you'd want to see me.

LOU: You could have just come over.

PETE: I thought you wouldn't want that.

LOU: You could have just come.

PETE: I'm sorry. I've nearly rung you so many times. I wanted to pull my life back together first, wanted to have something to offer.

LOU: What? A move to Dubai?

PETE: Well, if you wanted it, yeah.

LOU: What the fuck would I do out there? That's not gonna happen, Pete.

PETE: A new life, new start. Isn't that the best thing could happen to you right now?

LOU: I don't need it. I don't need you going away again, I couldn't deal with it.

PETE: You wouldn't have to if you came with me.

LOU: Pete.

PETE: Nothing changed between us, did it? Why wouldn't you want to pick back up where we left off?

LOU: I was pregnant, Pete. When you went in. I didn't know, I found out later. And I lost her when Dad was ill.

PETE: Oh my God.

LOU: I miscarried.

PETE: I didn't know about this.

LOU: I didn't know how to tell you.

PETE: Oh my God.

LOU: I told Ryan not to tell you. I wanted to do it myself, you know, just didn't know how we'd ever get onto it.

PETE: I can't believe I left you on your own to go through that.

LOU: It wasn't your fault.

PETE: I can't believe I wasn't there for you. I'm so sorry.

LOU: It wasn't your fault.

PETE: We would have had a kid?

LOU: Yeah. Well, no, but –

PETE: I would have loved that.

LOU: Really?

PETE: Is that the wrong thing to say? I'm sorry, that's the wrong thing to say.

LOU: No, it's –

PETE: Please come back to me, Lou. Please don't tell me that and say I can't be there for you.

LOU: I don't know, I don't know where I'm at. I'd love us to still be together. You were the best thing ever happened to me. But that was – I don't know whether you'd leave me again. What would I do if that happened again?

PETE gets down on one knee.

PETE: What if I asked you to marry me?

LOU: Fuck off.

PETE: Why not?

LOU: Don't be cruel.

PETE: Let's unbreak it. Let's unbreak it. *(Sings.)* 'Whatever I said, whatever I did, I didn't mean it, I just want you back again, want you back, want you back, want you back for good'. Yeah? Louise Katherine Mason, will you marry me?

LOU: You're such an idiot. You haven't got a ring.

PETE: You always said I wasn't spontaneous. We can get a ring later. Come on.

LOU: Are you serious?

PETE: Why not? I won't leave you alone, Lou. I don't wanna leave you alone.

LOU: Tonight is not the night.

PETE: Yeah, but it looks like it actually is though, doesn't it.

Silence.

PETE: I'll sing again.

LOU: Don't. Ask me properly.

PETE: Again?

LOU: I wanna get the feeling, I haven't had the feeling.

PETE: Shit, are you gonna say yes?

LOU: Just fucking ask me.

PETE: All right. Will you marry me?

Silence.

PETE: This is like the end of *Bake Off.*

LOU: You're such a dick. All right.

PETE: Yeah?

LOU: All right.

PETE: Fuck yes!

PETE gets up, kisses her, lifts her up.

LOU: Put me down!

PETE: You're really up for this?

LOU: Yes.

PETE: Sure you're sure?

LOU: Stop asking or I'll change my mind.

PETE puts her down. They look at each other.

LOU: Is this why you came over? This can't be what you planned to do.

PETE: No. I think I've just ended up going nuclear, haven't I.

LOU: Why is marrying me like a bombing?

PETE: It's not. I'll look after you, you know.

LOU: Yeah. I'll look after you too.

Enter RYAN.

RYAN: Erm, sorry. Did I just see what I think I just saw?

PETE: You did, yeah. I think you did.

RYAN: Oh my God.

PETE: I know right?

RYAN: Oh my God.

LOU: You all right with that bro?

RYAN: This is the fucking best thing ever.

PETE: Yeah?

RYAN: This is how it was supposed to be. We're back together. Fuck all that shit, we've come through it! We are fucking musketeers!

PETE: Yeah!

RYAN: You could move in with us.

LOU: Yeah.

RYAN: Fucking musketeers, mate, this is amazing. This is the fucking band back together!

LOU: Deep breaths Ryan.

RYAN: We gotta tell Mum.

LOU: Yeah?

RYAN: It'll be all right.

PETE: Give her a drink first maybe?

RYAN: Hang on, let me get her, Mum! Mum!

RYAN exits. PETE and LOU look at each other.

PETE: I didn't quite get in the bit about Dubai.

LOU: No, I noticed.

PETE: Gotta talk it through anyway.

LOU: Yeah, exactly.

PETE: Great. He'll be all right I reckon.

Act Two

SCENE ONE

A week later. Afternoon. Round the back of the house. RYAN is bricklaying, shirt off in the heat. PETE and LOU are watching. JENNY is idly inspecting the septic tank. By the septic tank are a pile of uncut logs and an axe stuck in one of the logs. A note – the thing about cement is that once it's mixed, it needs using, or it sets and you have to chuck it away. So RYAN will have to keep working hard through this scene.

JENNY: Do you two wanna come to *Mamma Mia* with me?

LOU: Is it at the Mayflower?

JENNY: No, London trip. Ryan doesn't want to, he's too miserable.

RYAN: It's a rip off.

JENNY: It's a joyous timeless thrilling experience and you can catch the last train home.

LOU: How much are tickets?

JENNY: You can get 'em for fifty quid I think.

LOU: Nah, you're all right.

JENNY: Don't be miserable, you can afford it.

LOU: Fifty plus trains and dinner?

RYAN: Rip off.

JENNY sings 'Mamma Mia'

JENNY: 'Mamma mia, here I go again, My my, how can I resist you?' How can you not want to experience that for real?

LOU: We've got the DVD.

JENNY: All right, forget it.

57

LOU: Let's see what's on at the Mayflower.

JENNY: Well you get free food poisoning thrown in there if you eat before the show, so if it's value you're looking for –

PETE: Did you get food poisoning at the Mayflower?

RYAN: No, I did. Went to Al Murray, had the prawns.

JENNY: I just thought we might like a day out in London.

LOU: Maybe.

JENNY: Now we're going to be so rich.

RYAN: You won the lottery then?

JENNY: No, but you keep telling me there's going to be so much money. Why not spend it on fun?

RYAN: I'd rather spend it on essential maintenance.

JENNY: And stupid hobbies that waste all your time.

RYAN: This is a good idea, just go with it.

JENNY: A good idea like when you thought you'd cut up all those logs last week?

RYAN: This is when you ought to cut logs. Fix the roof while the sun's shining.

JENNY: But you haven't fixed the roof, have you. You've just left an axe and a pile of bits of tree trunk in the middle of the lawn.

RYAN: I'll get it done. It's just a bit harder than it looks, that's all.

PETE: What you doing?

RYAN: Extension, innit.

PETE: Yeah?

JENNY: Making the back bedroom bigger. So we can Airbnb.

LOU: Try not to sound too excited about it.

JENNY: If it means the kitchen's bigger we can try your little schemes, as long as it doesn't take up my whole life changing sheets, you can do whatever.

PETE: This'll all be the kitchen then?

RYAN: When this is done I'm gonna knock through there, yeah. And the upstairs bedroom gets a second window, double aspect, we'll rent that out, hundred quid a week or whatever.

LOU: More light.

RYAN: Yeah.

PETE: Did you need planning permission?

RYAN: Nah, they were fine.

PETE: Really?

RYAN: Said it was OK, yeah, I called 'em up about it.

LOU: The planning office just said it was OK, over the phone, just like that?

RYAN: Yeah.

JENNY: I've only just realised that's a lie isn't it.

RYAN: No.

JENNY: You cheeky sod. I bet this does want planning permission, I bet you haven't called anyone at all.

LOU: Please don't say you've just started without telling anyone.

RYAN: It's our property, what does it matter? It's so far from the road no one's ever gonna see. Thanks mate.

PETE: Sorry.

JENNY: I can't believe you Ryan, you're so bloody slapdash.

RYAN: No, it's fine.

PETE: If you ever sold up, might have a problem, they can make you take stuff down.

RYAN: This'd be fucking brilliant if we sold up, adds value. More space. More light. More money.

LOU: But the surveyor would notice the change.

RYAN: They'd be all right about it.

JENNY: Well we're not about to sell our home I don't think, so perhaps it's not important. Maybe Ryan's right. It's our place. We'll do what we want with it.

RYAN: Thank you.

LOU: Mental.

JENNY: Englishman's home is his castle. If he wants to dig a moat then what's the problem?

LOU: Right.

RYAN: I don't think we want a moat though.

LOU: I've been making home improvements too.

JENNY: What have you done?

LOU: Replaced every door in the house with bead curtains. No, it's all right. Been having a clearout.

JENNY: Oh yeah?

LOU: Bagging up old stuff in the attic I don't need.

JENNY: I couldn't do that.

RYAN: No, that's why the house is full of rubbish.

JENNY: Memories, Ryan, not rubbish.

LOU: I've taken down all my posters. That was proper existential, that.

RYAN: You throw 'em all away?

LOU: No, they're rolled up in elastic bands. I've put them in the attic where the old stuff I don't want used to live. There's a category of thing you own, isn't there, that's stuff you don't want, but can't throw away, and just sort of keep in the garage.

RYAN: Basically describes everything you ever bought, Mum.

LOU: It'd be quite a good art exhibition. If everyone had to put the stuff they keep in cupboards on display, and be summed up by that. The things we hide and not the things we show.

JENNY: I don't know why you didn't go on with your art. You were good at it.

LOU: Not really.

JENNY: You had imagination.

LOU: I probably still have.

PETE: Me and Ryan did half your GCSE Art coursework.

LOU: Pete!

PETE: You made us do all those drawings of trees cos you said you were too busy.

JENNY: Were those not yours? I liked those.

RYAN: That was me had all the imagination then, wasn't it.

LOU: Lots of artists get other people to do the work for them. It's having the idea that counts.

PETE: I don't think you can claim that drawing a picture of a tree was your idea.

LOU: Well no, that had been done before, that's true.

JENNY: I can't believe you cheated your exams.

PETE: Nothing wrong with that if you can get away with it.

JENNY: Oh, why am I not surprised.

PETE: What?

JENNY: You find a way to bring it up again.

PETE: Excuse me?

JENNY: It doesn't matter if you get away with it, I mean really. Everything's about your scam.

PETE: I wasn't –

JENNY: The trouble is that people don't get away with it. Not for ever. I looked it up online. There were two blokes got busted three years ago in Kent. Another bloke got caught down the road from here, back in 2012. And they got three years, four years, they went to prison. You're robbing the biggest company in the entire world, they're eventually going to notice.

PETE: That's why we hid the hose. We haven't nicked enough to register, they can't see anything if they fly a drone over. If we wanted them to find out we'd have to literally call the maintenance hotline and tell them to come round, you can't tell otherwise. People get caught if they're greedy. Not if they're smart.

JENNY: The biggest company in the world. It might last for a while, but I promise you, at some point it will stop being all right. We never even wanted the pipe here in the first place. Des only let them put it through here to piss off Geoff runs the next farm.

RYAN: Really?

JENNY: Wouldn't have it at all if he didn't hate Geoff Owen so much.

LOU: He didn't hate Geoff.

JENNY: Your Dad once spent a year collecting up every stone in the west field, and piling them up in a tractor trailer. Then at midnight that New Year's Eve he drove over to Geoff Owen's top field and emptied the trailer right in the middle of it. It's a wonder they never murdered each other. That pipe was just a way of doing Geoff out of a bit of rent, I wish we'd never gone for it.

RYAN: So putting the fucking thing in was basically a scam in the first place.

JENNY: No.

RYAN: It was trying to fuck someone over.

JENNY: The money helped as well.

RYAN: And the money's helping now, that's why I done it. I don't see how it's so much worse.

JENNY: I saw Lee Hardwick here this morning, is that what he was here for, buying oil?

RYAN: He bought a few cans, yeah.

PETE: You're selling it round?

JENNY: Piccadilly bloody Circus here some days.

RYAN: Just to four or five guys. And it's fucking working, innit, the money's coming in.

JENNY: If your Dad was around he'd pull the whole thing out by the root. Someone will talk, Ryan. Someone will talk and we'll all go to prison.

RYAN: Back off a bit Mum yeah?

PETE: People know they have to be confidential though, do they?

RYAN: Yeah, course.

PETE: Cause we're all in shit if it comes out.

RYAN: It won't come out. I have to get on with this or it'll set.

LOU: We wanted to talk to you about something actually, guys.

JENNY: Oh right?

PETE: Yeah, bit of a thing. Lou and me have been talking about our work, and about where we're gonna live.

RYAN: Have you heard the same thought I did?

PETE: What?

RYAN: Well. I know I only said it was a joke the other day, right. But I've been thinking. When this is done, and the house is bigger like that. Are we completely sure that it wouldn't be fucking brilliant for you guys to live here?

PETE: Oh right.

RYAN: Fucking lager nights we'd have, you know? I've been thinking it might be an option.

PETE: Right. OK.

LOU: We were actually gonna say something else though.

RYAN: OK.

LOU: Pete?

PETE: Yeah, sure. So the thing is that I've been offered a job in Dubai.

JENNY: Dubai.

PETE: Yeah. And Lou and me have been talking about it over the last week. And we think it's something I should accept.

JENNY: Right.

PETE: So we wanted to talk to you about it, today. Cos it's got implications, obviously.

RYAN: Like what?

JENNY: You're gonna move to Dubai?

LOU: Well maybe. I know it sounds big.

JENNY: Sounds?

LOU: I'm sorry I haven't talked about it with you both till now. But the thing is, we wanted to talk through all the options first off, just me and Pete. Cos we want this to be about us, the start of our marriage. Can you see that?

JENNY: Not that you're actually married yet.

LOU: No, but you can see how this will shape a lot about our relationship, can't you. Whether I stay here or go out there with him.

JENNY: You'd be a housewife. Just sit all day in the air con.

LOU: At first, when I got over there, I wouldn't have a job. But listen. What I'm doing now isn't, like, the dream job for me. I'm not doing it because I wanted to do it for ever. And now Pete and me are a thing again, aren't we. And that gives me options I didn't know I had.

RYAN: I can't fucking believe this.

PETE: Mate, I'm sorry.

JENNY: It's traditional, Pete, that a young man comes and talks to the family of a girl before he asks her to marry him.

LOU: Mum.

JENNY: Now I can understand why that didn't happen with you two, because this engagement was very spontaneous of course, you haven't even got a ring yet –

LOU: We will.

JENNY: And in this day and age people think it's old fashioned. So of course, I didn't mind that you didn't ask me first. But I would have expected you to come to me with this.

LOU: Why should he?

JENNY: The impact this will have on our family.

LOU: I'm an adult, Mum. You don't need to be kept in the loop about everything I do.

JENNY: I'm not asking for everything, I'm just thinking if you're going to move to another continent, that might be worth flagging in advance.

LOU: Which is what we're doing now.

PETE: The idea is that I'd go out on my own at first. Lou would follow a bit later. If she decides that's the right thing to do. I'll need some time anyway to rent us a proper place, I'm in a hotel at first.

RYAN: I was so looking forward to all of us hanging out again.

PETE: Yeah, I know. Me too. But just to say where I'm at, my position, I kind of couldn't see how to turn this job down.

JENNY: We get that, Pete. What I don't understand is why it means Lou has to give up her career.

LOU: It's hardly a career, Mum, it's photocopying.

JENNY: You do more than photocopying.

LOU: I like the idea of going somewhere else. I think it would be interesting.

JENNY: Away from us, from here.

LOU: I've bent over backwards to be here and do my bit.

JENNY: Is that how it was? I seem to remember you needing me.

LOU: Yeah, because I did, we all did.

JENNY: Guess you just don't need me any more.

RYAN: Mum.

JENNY: So it's off to the next adventure. No thought for your family, no need to discuss it with them, just book the flight and away you go, cos that's what you and your boyfriend fancy.

PETE: But this is what we're trying to do, we're trying to discuss it with you today, Jenny. We worked out things on our side, now we've come to you.

JENNY: You're trying to pull my family apart.

PETE: What?

JENNY: That's what's happening.

LOU: Mum.

JENNY: First you turn him onto all this – guerrilla DIY. Now you wanna take her away from here.

LOU: That's so unfair.

JENNY: Is it? Why would I want you anywhere near my daughter anyway when you've done time?

PETE: I think you're forgetting what actually happened.

JENNY: I'm not.

PETE: I went to prison for something he did.

JENNY: You were both there.

PETE: He threw the punch. I was just the one got caught on CCTV. He threw the fucking punch and you know it. I went to prison as a favour to him, because of what you were going through.

JENNY: You were identified, you went to prison because you got caught.

PETE: But I could have spoken up. I could have said what happened. Got a shorter sentence. I didn't do that, out of respect for my mate, out of respect for Lou, out of respect for what you were going through. And then your husband went and persuaded his mate in the police not to bother looking for anyone else anyway, so don't go holding that sentence over me, you owe me a fucking apology for it, I ought to be thanked.

LOU: Dad did what?

PETE: You know this story better, Jenny, tell it.

JENNY: I don't remember anything about this.

PETE: Yes you do.

JENNY: It was a traumatic time.

RYAN: You know Kev Holland, knew Dad from school?

LOU: Yeah?

RYAN: Dad took him drinking. Kev said he'd wrap up the case.

PETE: What, you knew too?

RYAN: Sorry, yeah.

PETE: I thought they kept you out of it.

RYAN: I'm sorry.

LOU: Fucking hell.

RYAN: We didn't tell you Lou cos obviously for you it's complicated.

LOU: Why wasn't Dad trying to get you both off?

RYAN: You couldn't see my face on the CCTV. They had proper footage of Pete.

LOU: But he just said he didn't do it.

RYAN: That's not how I remember it.

PETE: Seriously? Don't you fucking dare mate.

A beat.

RYAN: Sorry. I'm sorry.

PETE: Fucking hell.

LOU: So it was you hit that kid?

RYAN: Yeah.

LOU: I gave up a year of my fucking life to come back here and look after you two.

JENNY: Pete was already going to prison, your dad saved who he could.

LOU: He saved family and drew the line at anyone else.

JENNY: They had him on the camera.

LOU: A fucking year I looked after you.

JENNY: How would we have told you? What would you have wanted us to say? What difference would it have made anyway?

RYAN: Pete...

PETE: I wish you'd told me you knew.

RYAN: I'm sorry.

PETE: You should have been up front about it. I might have understood if you were up front.

RYAN: You can understand now though, can't you?

PETE: I dunno. I wish you'd said.

RYAN: What was I supposed to do, Pete? Call up the station and hand myself in?

PETE: I thought I was protecting you. That was what your dad said, that was the deal. But you already knew.

RYAN: Mate, I'm sorry.

JENNY: Right. I want you to get off my land now, thank you.

PETE: What?

JENNY: I think you can go now, I want to talk to my children.

RYAN: Mum, don't be ridiculous.

JENNY: Can you get in your car and fuck off please? Do you think you could manage that for me?

PETE: All right, fine. Call me when you get out of here yeah?

LOU: Sure.

JENNY: Why does she need to get out of here?

PETE: Can I just say, before I go, and I'll go if you want, but I think you're making a joke of yourself. I think you're lying to yourself. If you think this place was all fine and I've fucked it, you're deluded. Your kids are so unhappy. You can't see that. But I care about them, so I can.

JENNY: Don't tell me I don't care about my kids.

PETE: You care about yourself, they're lifestyle appendages. All of this is just outfits you've collected to wear. I've always tried to be nice to you, Jenny, but you're being ridiculous.

JENNY: Of course, I'm ridiculous. And you're the one who's in the right. That's what children always think.

PETE: You should try and wake yourself up because your kids are gonna have to get away from this toxic fucking place if you don't change it. I've said my bit. Call me later.

PETE exits.

LOU: How could you let him sit in prison all that time?

RYAN: I didn't get any say. You know what Dad was like. When he'd made his mind up.

LOU: I stopped visiting. I can't believe it. You put someone in a wheelchair.

RYAN: I was off my nut. I'd been drinking all day.

LOU: So you hit someone.

RYAN: I'm not fucking proud of it all right?

JENNY: Ryan had much more to lose, you have to see the big picture Lou.

LOU: What?

JENNY: Des needed Ryan to be around to take over the farm. This is his life. If Ryan hadn't been around, what would have happened to it?

LOU: Ryan didn't even want the fucking farm.

RYAN: That's not true.

LOU: Neither of us wanted anything to do with all this shit. This is just the place where Dad died, this isn't our lives. Ryan didn't fucking want it.

JENNY: Maybe when you were first getting to grips with what you were taking over, maybe you did feel quite daunted by that. But I think Ryan has the maturity to recognise that there are things bigger than him that he needs to take responsibility for. This family will go on after he's gone, this is bigger than him.

LOU: That's bullshit. It's his life. You don't like it here. Tell her.

RYAN: Lou.

LOU: How could you want that for him? Look at him. How could you want him to feel like that?

JENNY: I don't know what you're talking about. I think we all spend a lot of time dancing round the jealousy you feel for your brother –

LOU: Excuse me?

JENNY: We all spend a lot of time putting up with your moods, your negativity about this place, which I think we all know springs really from you feeling hurt that it's not you who's in charge of it.

LOU: I'd have run a mile Mum.

JENNY: I wish you saw it clearer. Because you're not disinherited, you're so not, but the way you act all the time –

RYAN: I don't think that's fair at all.

JENNY: Really?

RYAN: I think Lou's done everything to help me get to grips with all the shit that comes with being here.

JENNY: Can you both stop telling me my life was shit?

Silence.

LOU: What?

JENNY: I'm sorry you don't like it. I'm sorry it's hard. I'm sorry if it's not what you dreamed of, what you wanted. But that, actually, is what life is like. That's one of the lessons you learn by growing up. Some of life is shit, and some of it you'll have to work hard at, and some of it won't be rewarding. I'm sorry that's come as a shock to you. Clearly we didn't teach you enough about that. But I think it's worth doing the hard bits because sticking at them is how you push through to the bits of life that matter. Like this place. This matters. Because it's the place where our whole lives have happened, all three of us. I can see myself, nineteen years old, hiding behind that tree, twenty-four years old, filling a basket with those apples. I can see you cutting your thumb on that pampas grass. I can see you following me out to the peg line, when you were barely walking. Our whole lives are here, and I'm sorry you have to get up early in the mornings, but that's part of the price you pay for holding onto all this.

RYAN: No one's saying it's not good us being here.

JENNY: That's all you ever say to me, you two. Everything you do I see it. You think you're miserable. You think you're cursed. You can't see how wonderful some of this is.

RYAN: We've all got a lot to get over, I don't think you can expect us to be skipping and jumping.

JENNY: No. But I don't see why you have to spend your whole time trying to twist the knife and make me feel guilty for having given birth to you.

LOU: That's mental. You should see someone, that's mental.

JENNY: Is it.

LOU: Seriously Mum, if you think that, you ought to get help.

JENNY: Don't go with him.

LOU: How could I stay after what I've just heard? You both lied to me for so long.

JENNY: But is this something you actually want?

LOU: I dunno.

JENNY: Well then.

LOU: I sometimes feel like I'm getting the bends. One minute I was just a kid in college. Then you're not allowed to be that any more. So they tell you you need money, so you find yourself a job. And all of a sudden your ambitions reduce down to that little world, and you find yourself chasing your Christmas bonus, chasing a rise, and you don't think about all the things you thought that you were gonna do when you were younger. You don't have a dream so you just go after money, cos at least that's something you can count. At least maybe you'll buy a house with it, or something like that, and that might count for something when they add you up. And suddenly you're twenty-eight and where's that gone, what happened to that? I'm going too fast through it and I'm getting crushed. I never had time to think about how to be happy. I never had time to work out whether I wanted the things that were happening to me, they happen so quickly, then they're gone. I don't want this feeling any more. I just want to feel like I'm choosing what happens to me.

JENNY: You don't sound to me like you're happy with him at all.

73

LOU: I'm not happy with anything, Mum. Everything I've got fucking sucks. But if I can change parts of it, I'll try that. And maybe that will make things better. So that's what I'm going to do, I'm going to try changing.

JENNY: And marry the kind of guy who takes you ring shopping in H.Samuel?

LOU: We weren't gonna buy the ring there. We were just coming up with ideas.

RYAN: I'm gonna be so gutted when you go.

LOU: You don't have to stay, you know. You could leave here.

RYAN: Yeah –

LOU: You don't actually owe anyone anything, Ryan. Not Dad, not Mum. And the world has other places in it.

RYAN: All right.

JENNY: Sometimes you're just as jealous of your sister as she is of you, I think.

RYAN: What am I jealous of?

JENNY: Well. She's got Pete.

RYAN: Scuse me?

JENNY: I do understand it, Ryan. I'm trying to tell you, you can talk to me about it. I know that it's hard for you.

A beat.

RYAN: I need to get on with work.

RYAN goes back to bricklaying.

JENNY: We don't have to talk about it now, but just know, I do get it, and I'm here for you.

LOU: What are you talking about? You just want him to feel like shit.

JENNY: No.

LOU: You want us to feel like shit so we need you.

JENNY: That's not true.

LOU: You thought it'd be the best thing that ever happened, Dad dying. Cos you'd get to be the centre of the world, like a little child. You can't bear that we have our own grief, our own lives, our own ways of coping.

JENNY: How dare you say that to me.

LOU: It's convenient for you to be able to turn him into a saint. And forget that he was a bully as well as the good things, and shit with money along with the good things, and flew off the handle, and tried to control. Now he's not here you can have the perfect husband.

RYAN: All right Lou, that's a bit fucking much, yeah? Shall we calm down a bit?

LOU: I hate this place so much, you know that? If I had my way, a year from now it wouldn't exist. I'd sell it to work, and they'd build on it. They'd tear that house down and put twenty identical new builds over the top, so you couldn't even make out the foundations. And everyone would forget about this life, it would be like it never existed. I'd like to see it buried so deep underground. That's how I'd remember him. That's how I'd remember him, I'd move on.

LOU exits. They watch her go. RYAN walks away from his work.

JENNY: Ryan? Ryan?

SCENE TWO

Early evening. A week later. Night will fall across the course of the scene. JENNY sits on stage in a deck chair round the side of the house, with a big gin and tonic. She has the Bluetooth speakers. Fleetwood Mac's 'The Chain' starts. RYAN enters with his gun. JENNY stops the song.

RYAN: Bit early?

JENNY: After four.

RYAN: Maybe not then. Might have one myself.

JENNY: Don't use my Fever Tree. Why you got that out?

RYAN: Crows. Passes the time.

Enter LOU and PETE from the house, carrying boxes.

RYAN: You packing the car?

LOU: Getting there, yeah.

RYAN: I'm sorry, I would have helped.

LOU: There's still more up there if you want.

RYAN: All right. You wanna come with, Mum?

Silence.

PETE: Guess not then.

RYAN exits towards the house, leaving the gun and bullet box on the bench as he goes. PETE exits towards the car.

LOU: Actually this one's ridiculous.

JENNY: Why?

LOU: School stuff, and – I don't even know. I don't need to take it all with me.

JENNY: Leave it here then.

LOU: Not cos I don't care about it. I just won't need it over there.

JENNY: What's in it, what school?

LOU: Year eleven I think.

JENNY: Let me see?

LOU puts the box down by JENNY. JENNY pokes through it.

JENNY: Oh, look. Oh leave that here with me.

LOU: Why?

JENNY: Let me have a look through all that, that's – I'll put it in the attic later.

LOU: All right. Nearly done now.

JENNY: Yeah?

LOU: Couple more loads and we're done. It'd mean a lot to me if you and Pete could make up a little bit, before we go. I don't want bad feeling. I don't think there has to be any, really.

JENNY: I'll talk to him.

LOU: Will you?

JENNY: I wanted to anyway.

LOU: Thank you.

JENNY: What will you do for your dinner tonight?

LOU: Probably get a Chinese.

JENNY: Lovely.

LOU: What about you?

JENNY: I've got that vegetable soup still left over, I think we'll have that.

LOU: Well I'll see you tomorrow at the airport then. If you wanna come?

JENNY: If you're really going, I'll be there. If you're really going, I'll wave you off.

LOU: OK.

JENNY: Gimme a hug.

They hug.

JENNY: I love you darling.

LOU: Love you too Mum.

Enter PETE.

LOU: I was just saying we'll be off in a minute, won't we.

PETE: Guess we're nearly done, yeah.

LOU: So. I'll get another box I think.

PETE: All right. I'll follow you up in a minute.

LOU: Oh right.

PETE: All good. See you in a minute.

LOU: OK.

LOU exits.

PETE: All right?

JENNY: Hard thing, moving out of a house, isn't it. You leave a lot of things behind you didn't know you weren't going to be able to take with you.

PETE: Yeah. Before we go I thought I should check we were all right?

JENNY: You and me?

PETE: I know it's upsetting, Lou leaving.

JENNY: Yes.

PETE: And I know we haven't really talked since last week. I've felt like you didn't wanna hear from me.

JENNY: That's about right, yeah. But it's fine. You won. That hurts. It's fine.

PETE: Well as long as we're all right going forwards.

JENNY: You've always been good with both my children.

PETE: I feel very lucky I'm marrying Lou.

JENNY: So you should.

PETE: I'm sorry if I've caused a bit of tension between you and Ryan.

JENNY: There's no tension between Ryan and me.

PETE: That's great. I'm only saying, I don't want to be the cause of any aggro. If you ended up chasing him away.

JENNY: I don't think that's about to happen.

PETE: That's great you think that.

JENNY: I'm so lucky to have someone around who knows my kids so well, and can tell me what they're thinking.

PETE: I'm sorry I've offended you.

JENNY: You're going to be part of my family, but I'd be grateful if you left my business to me, all right? I think I have the right to feel what I feel, and speak as I choose to.

PETE: All right.

JENNY: Thank you.

PETE: Once we're gone, though. And things have settled. I do think it'd be worth your while taking some time to think about the way you've behaved this last week.

JENNY: Do you.

PETE: Yeah, I do. And the whole last year, actually Jenny, if I'm honest. I think it'd be good if you thought about who it is you put first. Cos I don't think it's Lou or Ryan very often. And I think they've actually deserved that. I think they've needed that. And haven't got it. Might be good to think about that.

JENNY: I see.

PETE: I'll leave you to it.

PETE turns to leave.

JENNY: And what are you going to do about that?

PETE: What? Oh.

JENNY: Just walking away from it, are you? Not your problem now you're out of here.

PETE: It's working fine.

JENNY: But you'll leave him with the risk of being discovered.

PETE: Ryan's all right. He can keep his head down. What else could I do?

JENNY: Well you could take it apart again.

PETE: It's working fine.

JENNY: Or I could call the police I spose, get them to take it apart. I probably shouldn't, course, you're still on parole, aren't you. So that would actually affect you quite severely.

PETE: What are you doing, Jenny?

JENNY: You're not having my daughter, you little piece of shit. You're not talking to me like that. We let you spend half your childhood here, when you could have been on that shit estate. We cooked you dinner when your mum couldn't be fucked. We gave you more than anyone else has ever given you, you are not going to talk to me like that.

PETE: What are you going to do?

JENNY: If she leaves this farm tonight, I'll call Kev and tell him exactly what you've done. If she sets foot off this farm.

PETE: It's too late, Jenny.

JENNY: You have to tell her. Tell her you've changed your mind.

PETE: I'm not gonna do that.

LOU and RYAN enter, carrying boxes,

LOU: This is the last of it, I reckon. You two all right?

JENNY: Fine.

LOU: You sure you don't mind keeping all that stuff in the loft?

JENNY: Of course not, that's fine.

LOU: Thanks. I guess this is us, then.

JENNY: Unless you had anything you wanted to say, Pete?

PETE: Jenny.

LOU: What's the problem?

PETE: You shouldn't do this.

JENNY: Fuck you.

LOU: Mum!

PETE: Jenny says she's gonna call the police. If I take you away this evening. And tell them about the pipe.

LOU: Fuck's sake.

JENNY: He is not your life, Lou. You're making a mistake.

RYAN: Mum, shut up, please.

JENNY: Ryan.

RYAN: All you're doing is pushing her away. It doesn't even work.

JENNY: She needs to hear it.

RYAN: If you called the police I'd just say I did it.

JENNY: I wouldn't let you. They wouldn't believe you.

RYAN: I bet they would. It wouldn't even work, Mum, stop fucking up.

LOU: I have to go.

JENNY: Lou.

LOU: No, Mum, you've blown this. This was meant to be when we said goodbye, this was meant to be friendly. I can't believe you. Don't come to the airport tomorrow, all right? I don't want to see you.

JENNY: No.

LOU: Ryan, I'll see you tomorrow before we fly.

RYAN: All right.

LOU: I'll be in the car.

PETE: Yeah.

JENNY: Please.

LOU: No, Mum, not now.

LOU exits. JENNY breaks down in tears.

PETE: Hey. Hey, Jenny.

PETE kneels down next to her.

PETE: I'm sorry.

JENNY: Get off me.

PETE stands.

PETE: Gonna miss you mate.

RYAN: Me too. I'm sorry.

PETE: All done now.

RYAN: Remember the first time you ever came round here? Year seven. And your mum was an hour late to pick you back up, and it rained, and you wouldn't wait inside in case

she didn't see you. So we stood under that tree and took
turns playing *Pokemon Blue.*

PETE: Yeah.

PETE: *(He gestures to the pipe.)* You sure you know what you're
doing with that?

RYAN: I'm fine.

PETE: And if anyone does find out –

RYAN: It's fine. No one else needs to have been involved.

PETE: You sure?

RYAN: Be my turn anyway, won't it. To go down for
something. I'll be all right. I don't need my hand held, it's
all right.

PETE: See you at the airport then.

RYAN: All right.

PETE exits.

RYAN: Mum you are a fucking prize idiot.

JENNY: She didn't really mean I can't come to the airport, do
you think?

RYAN: I don't know, Mum. I think she might have done.

JENNY: Maybe you could call her. Call her in a few hours and
see if I can come.

RYAN: Maybe.

JENNY: Or in the morning.

RYAN: All right, all right.

RYAN: She was always gonna move back out one day.

JENNY: Never thought it'd be Dubai though. I thought more
Basingstoke or Southampton.

RYAN: I think we ought to meet with Lou's firm about that offer they made us.

JENNY: Oh.

RYAN: I think I'd like do that, if that's OK with you.

JENNY: Ryan.

RYAN: The bank want to repossess us, Mum. I know you won't talk about it, I know you'd rather pretend it's not happening, but they want to shut it all down. Maybe it's time to stop hiding away from that, start coming up with a plan.

JENNY: We'll turn the corner.

RYAN: People don't get out of our kind of debt just by grafting. You must know that. Don't you know that? We're in too deep, Dad left us in so deep. Eighty grand on credit cards alone, Mum.

JENNY: So you're pissed your mate left and now it's your father's fault?

RYAN: I didn't say that. How long do you keep doing something that makes you unhappy before it's time to change?

JENNY: Everything we could possibly do would make us unhappy right now. That's how grief happens. Like oil over everything. Drowning everything, all your life you see it through this slick. We have to keep going, that's all. We just have to keep going and believe we'll come out of this feeling.

RYAN: I'm really sorry, but I think I might have stopped believing that. I don't think you can live all your life saying the reason you're unhappy is something that happened last year. When maybe the problem's what's happening now, and you could change it if you only lifted up your head. I never thought about doing anything other than this, always thought this place would be my life. But look at what Lou's doing. It's like she found a trapdoor, and now she's in another world, and she doesn't have to deal with any of this. She can just breathe out.

JENNY: You're overreacting cos your friend's gone away.

RYAN: What?

JENNY: If Pete doesn't like it, neither do you. You were the same about olives.

RYAN: Mum.

JENNY: It's not real, Ryan. What you're feeling, it's natural, everyone thinks they could be doing better. That's what it's like. You went somewhere else, you'd be just as unhappy.

RYAN: Would you want me to keep going if you knew for sure that I didn't want to be here?

JENNY: I never make you do anything. I've never made you do anything all your life. Just don't be stupid, Ryan, don't rush, don't do the wrong thing.

RYAN: I wish you wouldn't call me stupid. Dad used to call me stupid all the time. If he'd told me I was bright, maybe I would have been. I wish we'd sat down the day we got back from the wake and said what we really thought. I thought I was doing what he would have wanted, I wish I could ask him. How can someone be there one day and then just not exist the next? I don't even understand it. I think we've tried very hard not to think about what's happened, haven't we.

JENNY: Yes.

RYAN: And all let each other have our time.

JENNY: Yes.

RYAN: I know I haven't talked. I don't know how to talk about this stuff. But I think that's part of why Lou had to leave, though, don't you? It gets to feel like you can't breathe, doesn't it. Maybe it's time to breathe out, Mum. We can't live as if we think he might come back.

JENNY: I know.

RYAN: We can't keep doing things just for him.

JENNY: You know it will be the end? Of cooked breakfasts and hardback books, and wellingtons and life outdoors, and open fires, and family meals together. No more time with the view all around you. You know that will end.

RYAN: But he died, Mum. And maybe all that went with him.

JENNY: This is our home.

RYAN: No, home was a time when we were together. I'm gonna get a drink. D'you want another?

JENNY: Yeah.

RYAN: Then maybe we can start on dinner.

JENNY: All right.

RYAN: And can I call the developers in the morning?

JENNY: All right.

RYAN exits. A moment. Then…

JENNY: Oh, my love, they're going away from me. And no one sees how much it hurts. I wish you were here to hold us. I didn't know it would finish so fast. What a terrible thing it is to marry someone. And tell someone I will give all of my love to you, and you can have all of my spare time, I will plant the roots of my life in you, all in the sure and certain knowledge it will one day end. I did the wrong thing coming here. I shouldn't have let you bring me here, so stupid. You're not even hearing me now, are you. You're not listening to me, you're not listening!

JENNY walks over and picks up the rifle. She holds it up to the light. Then she takes aim and shoots the pipe. The pipe breaks. Oil starts rushing out of it, drenching JENNY. Enter RYAN, carrying wine.

RYAN: Mum.

RYAN puts down the wine and the glasses he's carrying, and rushes to her, trying to get hold of her.

JENNY shoots the pipe again.

RYAN: Mum, what are you doing?

RYAN has his arms around his mother. He has stopped her attacking the pipe. He gets the rifle out of her hands and chucks it away from her, and pulls her away from the pipe, which is raining oil onto the ground. JENNY cries, and collapses to the floor.

JENNY: I wish I could burn it away. I wanna give it chemo till it's all burned away.

RYAN: What the fuck have you done?

JENNY: Get them back. He needs to fix it, get them back. Call Pete and tell him to turn the car around.

RYAN: No, Mum, I'm not gonna do that. They've got out, I won't make them come back.

JENNY: Just call him.

RYAN: I won't.

JENNY: But look at it, we can't leave it like that.

RYAN: I know.

JENNY: So what are we going to do? Can you close that up?

RYAN: I don't know.

RYAN realises.

JENNY: Ryan?

RYAN: I'm gonna call the maintenance line.

JENNY: No.

RYAN: That's what we have to do. Is the number inside?

JENNY: They'll know what's been happening. They'll know what we've done.

RYAN: Yeah but that's what has to happen, Mum. Lou and Pete have gone now. And it's my turn.

JENNY: Please.

RYAN: It is, it's my turn.

JENNY: You can't.

RYAN: I think I want to. I've felt so fucking bad for so long. Maybe if I do something right, that'll help me.

JENNY: I'd be on my own.

RYAN: There's nothing to be done. They've gone now, they're free of it. Let's give them that. I'd better go in and find the number.

JENNY: Please.

RYAN: What would Dad have wanted?

JENNY: I don't fucking know. I'm so angry at him. How dare he go and die? I can't hear him any more.

RYAN: I know. Look at that, up there. That's the only star I know besides Orion. When I get scared I tell myself it might be Dad. And he's looking out for me. Pointing the way.

JENNY: Why that one?

RYAN: Cos that's the pole star. First star in the evening. That's how you know where north is.

END.